© 2004 by Barbour Publishing, Inc.

ISBN 1-59310-007-8

Cover image © Images.com

Scripture quotations marked KJV are taken from the King James Version of the Bible.

Scripture quotations marked NKJV are taken from the New King James Version. Copyright © 1979, 1980, 1982 by Thomas Nelson, Inc. Used by permission. All rights reserved.

Published by Humble Creek, P.O. Box 719, Uhrichsville, Ohio 44683

Printed in China.
5 4 3 2 1

To Racheal,

DREAM BIG

WITH GOD
ALL THINGS ARE POSSIBLE

Amber James

HUMBLECREEK
INSPIRATION FOR LIFE

CONTENTS

Graduation Day. 6

Bittersweet Good-bye. 13

The Journey Ahead. 20

Dream the Impossible. 27

Good Luck!. 35

DREAM BIG

GRADUATION DAY

Look at a day when you are supremely satisfied at the end. It is not a day when you lounge around doing nothing; it is when you have had everything to do, and you have done it.

MARGARET THATCHER

Learn while you're young and not while you're old,
that a good education is better than gold,
for silver and gold will all melt away,
but a good education will never decay.

ANONYMOUS

There will come a time when
you think everything is finished.
That will be the beginning.

LOUIS L'AMOUR

BIG DREAM

Learning is a treasure that will
follow its owner everywhere.

CHINESE PROVERB

Education sows not seeds in you,
but makes your seeds grow.

KAHLIL GIBRAN

The will to win, the desire to succeed,
the urge to reach your full potential. . .
these are the keys that will unlock the door
to personal excellence.

EDDIE ROBINSON

Success is never a destination—it is a journey.

SATENIG ST. MARIE

The great recipe for success is
to work and always work.

LEON GAMBETTA

You have achieved success if you have lived well,
laughed often, and loved much.

ANONYMOUS

DREAM BIG   9

DREAM
BIG

What you achieve through
the journey of life
is not as important as
who you become.

AUTHOR UNKNOWN

The value of achievement lies in the art of achieving.

ALBERT EINSTEIN

THE BIG DAY IS HERE

My brother's graduation ceremony was a memorable experience for me. I was delighted to share that eventful occasion with him.

When my parents and I arrived at the high school, we took our seats and waited for the ceremony to begin. I eagerly sat on the edge of my chair, anxious to hear my brother's name announced. "John James. . ." I perked in my seat and saw my brother stand. As he accepted his diploma, he looked up at us with a big grin.

My brother's achievements motivated me. I knew my graduation was steadily approaching, and I needed to make the most of my high school experience to ensure a secure future. With God by my side and in control of my life, I was filled with an overwhelming sense of peace about my own graduation.

BIG DREAM

Your schooling may be over,
but remember that your education
still continues.

AUTHOR UNKNOWN

Education is the most powerful weapon
you can use to change the world.

NELSON ROLIHLAHLA MANDELA

BITTERSWEET GOOD-BYE

Do not be dismayed at good-byes.
A farewell is necessary before you can meet again.
And meeting again, after moments or lifetimes,
is certain for those who are friends.

RICHARD BACH

DREAM BIG

DREAM
BIG

I did not ask for it to be over,
but then again,
I never asked for it to begin.
For that is the way it is with life,
as some of the most beautiful days
come completely by chance.
But even the most beautiful days
eventually have their sunsets.

ANONYMOUS

When one door closes,
another one opens,
but we often look so long and regretfully
at the closed door that we fail to see
the one that has opened for us.

ALEXANDER GRAHAM BELL

BIG DREAM

GOOD-BYE, MY FRIEND

The night was cold, although summer was upon us. My friend and I talked all night and exchanged several stories and memories. We reminisced about the day we first met in seventh grade and recalled old times spent together. Some stories made us laugh, and others brought tears to our eyes. Knowing we were both about to start new chapters in our lives, we hoped the hours of the night would pass slowly, so we could prolong our time together. . .however, the dawning sun soon peered at us over the horizon.

As we realized it was time for us to part, it seemed as though it was a dream. But we knew reality was the only element surrounding us. Our hugs and good-byes were emotional as we struggled to part from one another. As she made her way to the car, my friend turned and smiled, waving one last time as if to say everything would be okay. I watched her drive down the road until I lost sight of her car; then I made my way inside the house, attempting to control my emotions.

With a heavy heart, I looked out the window one last time. My eyes caught the glimmer of a beautiful rainbow in the sky. Suddenly, I felt God's presence. He gave me assurance that good-byes are necessary for us to move ahead in our lives and on to the future He has planned for each of us.

DREAM
BIG

Change is difficult
but often essential to survival.

LES BROWN

The first step toward change is awareness.
The second step is acceptance.

NATHANIEL BRANDEN

 Change is the law of life.
And those who look only to the past or present
are certain to miss the future.

JOHN F. KENNEDY

**Courage is
being afraid
but going on anyhow.**

DAN RATHER

It takes a lot of courage to release the familiar and seemingly secure, to embrace the new. But there is no real security in what is no longer meaningful. There is more security in the adventurous and exciting, for in movement there is life, and in change there is power.

ALAN COHEN

BIG DREAM

THE JOURNEY AHEAD

I am not afraid of tomorrow,
for I have seen yesterday,
and I love today.

WILLIAM ALLEN WHITE

The world of tomorrow belongs to
the person who has the vision today.

ROBERT SCHULLER

> "Be strong and of good courage,
> do not fear nor be afraid of them;
> for the LORD your God,
> He is the One who goes with you.
> He will not leave you nor forsake you."

DEUTERONOMY 31:6 NKJV

DREAM BIG

DREAM BIG

LIFE'S CROSSROADS

You are now at a crossroads. This is your opportunity to make the most important decision you will ever make.

Forget your past.

Who are you now?

Who have you decided you really are now?

Do not think about who you have been.

Who are you now?

Who have you decided to become?

Make this decision consciously.

Make it carefully.

Make it powerfully.

ANTHONY ROBBINS

Look at life
through the windshield,
not the rearview mirror.

BYRD BAGGETT

We know what we are,
but know not what we may be.

WILLIAM SHAKESPEARE

Nobody gets to live life backwards.
Look ahead—
that's where your future lies.

ANN LANDERS

23

BIG DREAM

GOD IS CONSTANT

When my friends and I turned eighteen, we had a great deal of freedom and responsibility—and at the same time, society expected us to be prepared for the future. We were all anxious, because the journey ahead of us was unknown. We knew that life after graduation was only the beginning of the rest of our lives.

Before my friends and I moved ahead in our lives, we realized one important fact: Although we had families and friends who loved us, God was the only One who remained constant. We could depend on Him when we could count on no one else.

This truth made our transitions less difficult. We knew that no matter where life took us, God was our security. He never let us down once we put our trust in Him.

Yesterday is
but today's memory,
and tomorrow is
today's dream.

Kahlil Gibran

My interest is in the future because
I am going to spend the rest of my life there.

Charles F. Kettering

DREAM BIG

We must never be afraid to go too far,
for success lies just beyond.

MARCEL PROUST

Change in all things is sweet.

ARISTOTLE

DREAM THE IMPOSSIBLE

And Jesus looking upon them saith,
With men it is impossible, but not with God:
for with God all things are possible.

MARK 10:27 KJV

BIG DREAM

Dreams

Hold fast to dreams
For if dreams die
Life is a broken winged bird
Afraid to fly
Hold fast to dreams
For if dreams go
Life is a barren hill
Covered with snow

LANGSTON HUGHES

When we are motivated by
goals that have deep meaning,
by dreams that need completion,
by pure love that needs expressing,
then we truly live life.

GREG ANDERSON

A successful person is a dreamer
whom someone believed in.

AUTHOR UNKNOWN

DREAM BIG

I can do all things through Christ
who strengthens me.

PHILIPPIANS 4:13 NKJV

Successful people are not gifted;
they just work hard
and then succeed on purpose.

G. K. NIELSON

Happy are those who dream dreams
and are willing to pay the price
to make them come true.

ANONYMOUS

The future belongs to those who believe
in the beauty of their dreams.

ELEANOR ROOSEVELT

Yes, you can be a dreamer
and a doer too,
if you will remove one word
from your vocabulary:
IMPOSSIBLE.

ROBERT SCHULLER

BIG DREAM

God Nurtures Our Dreams

Throughout my life, I wanted to become many things—among them, a ballerina, a librarian, and a teacher. My biggest ambition, though, was to prevail as a writer.

As I became more serious about writing, I took on a small project with my church youth group. I wrote a small skit for the group to perform in front of the congregation. I wasn't looking for a response, but numerous friends, family, and strangers took me aside after the program and told me I had a special talent.

"Are you considering journalism as a college major?" everyone asked.

I was unsure of my answer to that question, so that night I went to God in prayer. His plan for my life was not obvious in the beginning, but I never gave up hope. I believed He was working in ways I could not see, and my assumption was correct. My dreams soon became realities, and I began writing.

Once I placed my ambitions into God's hands, He made my journey worthwhile and showed me impossible dreams are indeed possible through Him.

DREAM BIG

Trust in the LORD with all thine heart;
and lean not unto thine
own understanding.
In all thy ways acknowledge him,
and he shall direct thy paths.

<small>PROVERBS 3:5–6 KJV</small>

Go confidently in the direction of your dreams.
Live the life you've imagined.

<small>HENRY DAVID THOREAU</small>

GOOD LUCK!

What lies behind us
and what lies before us
are tiny matters compared to
what lies within us.

AUTHOR UNKNOWN

DREAM BIG

What we are is God's gift to us.
What we become is our gift to God.

ELEANOR POWELL

BIG DREAM

DREAMS OF TOMORROW

Dreams come with rays of hope that tomorrow
   they might be fulfilled.
Each step taken is one step closer to our dreams.
Patterns change, and we evolve.
Trends come and go.
Yet dreams cannot be taken as lightly.
True dreams need the hope of the future
And time to find what moves our hearts.
Now is the time to start the journey
And satisfy the dreams of our soul.
Take each step carefully with God.
Slowly, as the steps have more movement,
Dreams of today become fulfilled tomorrow.

AMBER JAMES, 2003

Luck marches with those who
give their very best.

H. JACKSON BROWN JR.

The best thing about the future is
that it comes one day at a time.

ABRAHAM LINCOLN

We aim above the mark
to hit the mark.

RALPH WALDO EMERSON

DREAM BIG

When I am delivering my very best,
that is when I feel successful.

Art Fettig

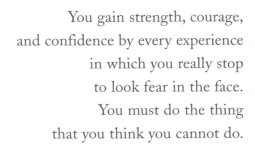

You gain strength, courage,
and confidence by every experience
in which you really stop
to look fear in the face.
You must do the thing
that you think you cannot do.

Eleanor Roosevelt

TODAY IS THE DAY

Now is the accepted time, not tomorrow,
    nor some more convenient season.
It is today that our best work can be done
    and not some future day or future year.
It is today that we fit ourselves for
    the greater usefulness of tomorrow.
Today is the seedtime; now are the hours of work,
    and tomorrow comes the harvest and the playtime.

AUTHOR UNKNOWN

BIG DREAM

CONGRATULATIONS, GRADUATE!

Dream the impossible—
for with God *all things* are possible.

Love and best wishes,
The Buechners